Come Ba
Light Refr
After the Service

A Play by

JULIE DAY

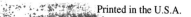

IMPORTANT BILLING AND CREDIT REQUIREMENTS

All producers of COME BACK FOR LIGHT REFRESH-MENTS AFTER THE SERVICE *must* give credit to the Author of the Play in all programs distributed in connection with performances of the Play and in all instances in which the title of the Play appears for purposes of advertising, publicizing or otherwise exploiting the Play and/or a production. The name of the Author *must* also appear on a separate line, on which no other name appears, immediately following the title, and *must* appear in size of type not less than fifty percent the size of the title type.

COME BACK FOR LIGHT REFRESHMENTS AFTER THE SERVICE was first presented by Field-Day Enterprises at the Carlton Courthouse Theatre on 6th February 1991. It was directed by Margaret Steven; the set realization was by Julie Day and the lighting was by Peta Hanrahan. Drawings and artwork by Sally Murray-White. The cast in order of appearance, was as follows:

SINGER	Wendy Ealey
REVEREND JAMES HEALEY	John Lavery
BETH	Fiona Kennan
ENID	Alethea McGrath
PAT	Julie Day
VANESSA	Marie Louise Walker

AUTHOR'S NOTE

Working as a member of a community House, it became obvious to me that the carers in our society are overlooked and undervalued.

Working as an actress, it became obvious to me that there is a lack of acting parts that portray women in worthwhile roles.

Working in the home kitchen, it became obvious to me that our women's conversation as we prepare the evening meal is a form of theatre, and I began to visualize the possibility of transferring my kitchen onto the stage.

The simple play that was thus created has a certain diversity in that it developed two texts—the dialogue and, by necessity, the action. I have decided, therefore, to include specific directions pertaining to the food preparation which occurs throughout the play. These appear in tandem with the appropriate dialogue and are offered to facilitate future productions.

I wish to acknowledge the help and support of all members of the original production without whom this play would never have been written.

Julie Day

THE CAST

BETH — in her mid-thirties, daughter of the deceased
REV. JAMES HEALEY — the family priest (Anglican)
ENID — a woman in her early seventies, life long neighbor
    of the deceased
PAT — a woman in her forties, and neighbor of Beth for
    fifteen years
VANESSA — a nineteen year-old niece of Pat's
A SINGER

THE SETTING

The Prologue takes place outside the church after the funeral.

The bulk of the action takes place in the kitchen and dining/
living area of Jack's home. Nothing post dates the fifties. The
kitchen table is framed by a return bench from the functional
sink, a round shouldered fridge, and a functional electric oven.
The home is clean but shows signs of wear. The artifacts evoke
memories of times gone by. A St Kilda Premiership poster is
displayed on the wall as is an up-to-date tea-towel calendar.
The living/dining area has a Victorian oval table and dresser
that have seen better days.

The Epilogue takes place at the graveside.

THE TIME

The present.

COME BACK FOR LIGHT REFRESHMENTS
AFTER THE SERVICE

*(EACH MEMBER OF THE AUDIENCE HAS BEEN SUP-
PLIED WITH A COPY OF THE ORDER OF SERVICE
AND A BLACK ARM BAND.)*

Prologue

(Singing of the 23rd Psalm.)
(BLACKOUT.)
*(BETH enters in Blackout and stands in space under spot.
Spots come up on BETH who is looking solemn and wear-
ing subdued clothing. REV. JIM enters and approaches her.)*

JIM. Well Beth — How are you feeling now?

BETH. Oh... ah. Thank you father. It was a lovely service.
It was just the way I hoped it would be, actually I... I just want
to thank you for doing everything the way I asked, I think it
all went very well. Ummm. I think it was just how Dad would
have wanted it.

(BETH goes into reverie.)

JIM. Are you all right?

BETH. A bit... you know... a bit strange.

JIM. Well yes, it is a bit of an ordeal isn't it? *(BETH does not respond. Uncomfortable pause.)* —Yes, well the mourning coach is waiting for us, so if you're ready we should make a move.

BETH. Look Father—I've decided I'm not coming. I don't want to go to the graveside service. I want to go home.

JIM. Oh? —Oh, of course. Well yes all right. I understand. *(He doesn't.)* Who's taking you?

BETH. I'll walk.

JIM. Are you sure you'll be all right?

BETH. Yes, I just need to have a breath of fresh air, and a bit of time to myself.

JIM. OK. Well then perhaps I should get going, the driver is waiting. Oh, perhaps I should give you these now—they're cards from the floral tributes.

BETH. *(Takes cards.)* Thank you. *(Stares at the cards abstractly and starts to leave then comes back to say...)* Oh, Father, when you've finished at the graveside could you please tell everyone that they're most welcome to come back to our... my place for light refreshments after the service.

Scene 1

(BETH enters the kitchen space and sheds extraneous clothes. She puts on the electric jug for tea. She sighs as in relief and chuckles to herself. Makes herself feel completely at home. Picks up floral tribute cards and shuffles them, lays them out on the table as in a solitaire game and then looks at some of them reading the messages. Comes across two

*identical cards, puts them down and says "snap" and laughs.
A real sense of freedom pervading all her actions.)*

*(PUTS TEA IN POT, MAKES CUP AND SAUCER READY, GETS MILK
FROM FRIDGE, POURS HOT WATER INTO POT AND PUTS COSY
ON POT BEFORE SITTING AT TABLE TO LOOK AT CARDS.)*

ENID. *(Off stage.)* Beth, Beth. It's me Enid. Can I come
in? You've left the front door wide open. Anybody could walk
straight in. *(ENID enters.)* Are you all right, dear?

*(ENID is carrying her hat, bag, order of service and a white
carnation.)*

BETH. Yes, yes. I'm fine.

ENID. Well then, what's happened? I was sitting in the
mourning coach, just waiting for you and Father Jim. But when
he came you weren't there. I looked around and saw you walking off. Well I jumped out of the car to see if you were all
right, but I couldn't cross the street until all the cortege had
passed. I thought something terrible had happened, so I came
as quickly as I could. What's wrong?

BETH. Nothing's wrong. I just decided I didn't want to go
to the graveside.

ENID. Not go and say your last good-bye? What will people
think? It's bad enough that your sister didn't fly home to pay
her last respects, now you won't go and see him to his final
resting place.

BETH. *(Calmly.)* Enid, come on, be fair, you know the last
time Frances came home Dad didn't have a clue who she was.
He hasn't even known who we are for the last few years.

(BETH packs up cards.)

ENID. That doesn't mean you shouldn't pay your last respects. Poor old Jack, he was always a good friend to me. I've lived next door to him for seventy-three years next August. Even when I was a little toddler, he was there and now he's gone off to his grave all by himself.

BETH. You can still get there in time, if you want to go.

ENID. Yes, yes I think I will go. *(She makes off then stops.)* But what about you—I can't leave you here all by yourself and acting so strangely. No, no, I'll stay here and make you a nice cup of tea. *(She takes off her hat and coat and puts down her bag.)* But what are people going to think? I've got to go to church on Sunday, and I'm sure I don't know what I'm going to say to everyone. It's so odd. Us disappearing like that. What your mother would've thought (God rest her soul) I don't know. Beth, since your mother died, I've tried to fill the gap. I think of you as a daughter. Heavens I've known you all your life, I used to change your nappies, but sometimes I just don't understand you at all.

(DURING ABOVE, BETH TAKES HATS, COATS AND BAGS OFF STAGE. THEN GOES TO KETTLE AND POURS TEA. ENID SITS AT KITCHEN TABLE AND BETH GETS HER A CUP OF TEA.)

BETH. Here, Ee, here's a cup of tea. I reckon we'll have an hour or so before everyone comes back. That'll be plenty of time to get ready.

(BETH PUTS MILK IN FRIDGE.)

ENID. Oh heavens, yes I'd forgotten about that. But I thought Pat and young Vanessa were seeing to it. Pat's very capable but why she wants that giddy young niece of hers helping, I don't know.

(ENID puts carnation on the table.)

BETH. Vanessa'll be a great help. That catering firm she works for want her full-time as soon as she's finished her degree. God how time flies! It seems like only yesterday that she climbed the side fence, marched in here and said "Hello, I'm Vanessa and I'm sleeping at my Arnie Pat's." Funny how nicknames stick, she still calls Pat "Arnie".

(BOTH WOMEN DRINK TEA—BETH STANDING AT THE SINK.)

ENID. That's all very well but why aren't they here? They said they would be.

BETH. Pat's got a key, don't worry she'll have it all in hand. She doesn't know I'm home yet, remember.

ENID. Well I must be able to do something. What about these sandwiches? What do you want in them.

BETH. There's some cheese and celery, and curried egg in the fridge.

ENID. Right.

(ENID makes no effort to move. Instead she takes a sip of tea.)

PAT & VANESSA. *(Off stage ad-libbing and laughing.)* Ness, can you open the door— careful. Can you manage that? Sure etc.

(PAT AND VANESSA ENTER LADEN WITH FOOD AND PARAPHERNA-LIA.)

(As PAT and VANESSA enter PAT sees BETH.)

PAT. Beth, what are you doing here? Is it that late? I thought we had plenty of time.

BETH. You have. I've come back early.

PAT. What's happened, are you all right?

(The next five lines spoken by ENID, BETH, VANESSA, PAT, BETH overlap.)

ENID. I don't know what's wrong with her. She won't tell me.

(BETH PUTS HER CUP DOWN AND HELPS PAT UNLOAD. PUTS SCONE BASKET AND 2 LARGE TEAPOTS ON TOP OF FRIDGE.)

BETH. Yes, I'm all right, I just didn't want to go to the cemetery. I thought I'd rather be home here helping you all to get ready... I didn't see the point. Hi! Vanessa.

VANESSA. Hi Beth! Here?

(VANESSA indicates the bench.)

(VANESSA PUTS BREAD ON BENCH AND THE REST ON TABLE. ENID HELPS.)

PAT. I can understand that. Good, we can do with an extra pair of hands.

BETH. *(To VANESSA.)* Sure that's fine.

(VANESSA puts things down.)

PAT. Well here are the Scouts' teapots, we've already been in and put the pies in the warmer.

(PAT PUTS BASKET ON STOOL BESIDE STOVE.)

VANESSA. It's nice of the Scouts to do that for you.
BETH. She does plenty for the Scouts.

(PAT GIVES VANESSA APRON - FRENCH MAID IN SCANTY KNICKERS NOVELTY APRON. PAT PUTS BASKET ON FLOOR AND BOWL OF SCONE MIX ON STOOL.)

PAT. Now the boys are grown up I don't do that much. I'll turn the oven on. Oh great you've already greased your Mum's Gem Irons.
BETH. They're already greased and in the oven.

(ENID GOES TO SINK AND WASHES CUP.)

(The next three lines by PAT, VANESSA, PAT are overlapped.)

PAT. Good. Well, we've got sausage rolls, party pies,
VANESSA. ... sandwiches, a couple of cakes, dips and dry biscuits and the gem scones.
PAT. Do you think I should put out some of my Anzacs?
BETH. We probably won't need them, leave them and we'll bring them out if we run short.

(PAT PUTS GEM IRONS IN OVEN.)

(ENID DRIES HANDS.)

PAT. Oh Beth, seeing you're here will you ice the cakes you're much better at it than me.

(VANESSA GIVES ICING TO BETH. PAT PUTS ON APRON. ENID PASSES BREAD TO VANESSA. THEY OPEN BREAD BAGS TOGETHER.)

VANESSA. The icing only needs moistening. This is chocolate and here's the lemon. Enid could you pass me over some of the bread. How many do you think will be here? It's sort of hard to know isn't it? I mean for a wedding or a twenty-first its all clear cut R.S.V.P.'s and everything, but with this, well it's such short notice really isn't it? At least it's a nice day for it.

(VANESSA puts on risque apron.)

ENID *(Sees apron.)* Pat, tell Vanessa to take off that apron. This is a funeral not a French Farce. Have some respect.

PAT. Oh, Enid stop being so stodgy? Vanessa it's all right. Look Jack's dead, he's gone, what the hell does it matter what anyone wears. It's just as well he can't see you in it, he would have chased you round the kitchen!

ENID. You know Jack wasn't like that.

PAT. No, you're right. He wasn't. He was a gentleman of the old school He always lifted his hat when he saw you in the street, stood up for women in the buses. He was a lovely man.

(VANESSA SETS OUT PRE-BUTTERED BREAD ON BENCH. ENID SITS AT TABLE.)

(BETH ADDS WATER FROM ELECTRIC JUG TO ICING TO MOISTEN IT FOR SPREADING.)

ENID. And he was clever. He left school at fifteen but that didn't stop him working his way up. He got to be a bank manager, you know.

(BETH nods and smiles wistfully in agreement.)

PAT. (To BETH.) Are you all right?
BETH. Sure.

(PAT GETS SPOONS FROM BENCH DRAWER.)

PAT. Have you got any Brandy?
BETH. Honestly I feel fine.

(PAT THEN TAKES THE SPOONS TO STOVE.)

PAT. I didn't mean for you. I just thought it would be nice in a cream filling for the chocolate cake.
ENID. Poor old Jack. He used to love a chocolate cake.

(VANESSA TAKES BREAD BOARD AND KNIVES AND SETS THEM ON BENCH BESIDE BREAD. PAT TAKES PLASTIC WRAP OFF ASPARA-GUS ROLLS.)

BETH. Yes, he did. That was what I was baking when I first noticed there was something wrong with him. Frances was visiting us. He wanted to get to the stove. But she was standing in front of it. Well Dad said, "Enid, for God's sake get out of the way". We didn't take any notice. He said again,

"Enid, for God's sake get out of the way". Frances and I looked at each other and I said "Enid isn't here, Dad, who are you talking to?" He shook his fists and stamped his feet in frustration, pointed his finger at Frances and said: "That tart there". We laughed at the time because it was so unlike him and the chocolate cake got burnt. *(Pause.)* After that I started to notice he'd often get easily confused and frustrated.

(VANESSA GOES TO FRIDGE, TAKES OUT CHEESE AND CELERY FILL-ING AND GOES BACK TO BENCH A DRAWER.)

PAT. Christine Northey dropped in with this plate of as-paragus rolls. She said she was sorry to hear about Jack but she wouldn't come to the funeral. She said you'd understand. She asked me to keep her plate for her, and she'd pick it up one day next week. You know what that means? Another two hour D & M—God!

(PAT GOES TO DRESSER.)

ENID. *(Aside to VANESSA.)* What's D & M?
VANESSA. Deep and meaningful Enid.
BETH. Pat, why do you do it?
PAT. What can I do? —She just needs someone to talk to. The other day we had a six cup session.
BETH. You're a glutton for punishment.

(PAT TAKES TABLE CLOTHS FROM DRESSER.)

PAT. I think she's got the constitution of a camel. I was desperate for a pee by the time she left. Which one the stain or the hole?

(PAT shows BETH two tablecloths.)

BETH. The hole.

(PAT MOVES FLOWERS OFF TABLE.)

PAT. All I do is nod at the appropriate times and ask the standard questions like: What was it you wanted? or How do you feel about that? You know the sorts of things. Then she looked at her watch and said: "Oh, I'll have to go, I don't want to, I'm finding this discussion so valuable but I have to be at my psychiatrists in half an hour.

(BETH chuckles.)

BETH. What do ya reckon? Menopause?

(BETH IS MIXING ICING.)

ENID. Shhhh!
PAT. Probably.
BETH. How on earth did women cope with menopause before psychiatrists?

(PAT THROWS TABLE CLOTH OVER TABLE.)

PAT. They'd go and have two hour D and Ms... with their friends.
VANESSA. My mother has hormone replacement therapy. *(BETH and PAT exchange glances.)* Well I think it was very nice of Mrs. Watsername to bring the asparagus rolls.

ENID. It was part of the way of life for the older generation. Everyone used to furnish the funeral table. It was a token of respect. Nowadays people just put their hand in their pocket, buy flowers and think they've been generous.

(ENID GOES TO FRIDGE TO GET CURRIED EGGS. MOVES TOWARD VANESSA AND UNCOVERS THEM.)

VANESSA. Phew! What's that awful smell?
ENID. It's the curried eggs.
BETH. It smells a bit like Dad on one of his bad days.

(PAT PUTS ASPARAGUS ROLLS ON D TABLE.)

ENID. Beth!

(VANESSA IS CUTTING SANDWICHES.)

VANESSA. What do you mean?
ENID. *(Diverting the conversation.)* You know, I think you're right. A cream brandy filling for that chocolate cake would be lovely. I'll slip home. I've got a bottle of hospital brandy. I'll go and get it.

(ENID exits.)

PAT. Hospital Brandy hey!
BETH. *(Calls after ENID.)* Righto! *(To PAT and VANESSA.)* I have got brandy here but it's good to have her out of the house for a minute or two. I know she's well meaning but. I decided

not to go to the cemetery because I needed to come home and have a few minutes by myself. I'd just sat down and I could hear her coming up the path "Beth, Beth, are you all right?" She was in here before I could say anything, before I could hide under a chair. God, she really is too much at times.

(BETH GOES TO DRESSER. PAT GOES TO OVEN. THEY CROSS CEN-TRE STAGE. BETH PUTS CAKE SERVER ON TABLE AND TAKES 2 CAKE PLATES TO KITCHEN TABLE. PAT TAKES IRONS OUT OF OVEN AND BEGINS TO FILL THEM.)

PAT. She can be a bit hard to take.
BETH. I don't believe her.

(VANESSA TAKES PLATTER FROM TABLE TO BENCH.)

PAT. Well she thinks of you as a daughter, you see.
BETH. That's exactly my problem. She's been saying lots of things like, "I've tried to be a mother to you." I know she expects me to arrange her funeral and go through all the rig-marole for her.

(BETH TAKES DOILIES FROM K TABLE DRAWER AND PUTS THEM ONTO CAKE STANDS.)

VANESSA. Why would she expect you to do that? Well I mean you're not related to her, it's nothing to do with you. She's not your responsibility.
BETH. No, but she's known me all my life.
VANESSA. Yeah, so what? That's not enough reason for her to expect you to look after her.

BETH. She doesn't have anyone else. I've been doing it for the last five years for my father, why shouldn't I do it for her? That's how she sees it.

PAT. She's always helped with Jack. Well what she calls 'help'. And of course "one good turn deserves another."

(BETH FILLS BOWL WITH WATER FROM ELECTRIC JUG TO PUT ICING UTENSILS IN.)

BETH. Yes, well she did help—not as much as you but she tried. She looked after him a few times so I could have a night off.

VANESSA. How often did that happen?

BETH. Occasionally I'd need to get out of the place.

VANESSA. What—you mean you looked after him all the time? Wasn't there anyone helping you?

(BETH PUTS LEMON ICING ON CAKE.)

BETH. Well Pat helped. There was the district nurse and if I really needed help I could get meals on wheels or someone from the council. Mostly it was just Pat and me.

VANESSA. I don't know why you just didn't chuck him in a nursing home. I would have.

(VANESSA IS CUTTING SANDWICHES.)

BETH. No I couldn't do that. I did a couple of times when I went away. I had to get away for a week or so, just to have a break. He misbehaved so much I couldn't believe it. He decided he didn't want to wear any clothes in the nursing home so he walked round naked.

(PAT nods amusedly.)

VANESSA. Oh my God!

BETH. When the nurses tried to dress him he swore at them, apparently using language I didn't know he knew. They just laughed it off but I felt embarrassed just the same.

VANESSA. Did he know what he was saying?

(PAT and BETH answer together.)

PAT. No.

BETH. Who knows? One night he just wandered off and they couldn't find him anywhere, they tried the ground and the loos, all the obvious places. They thought they'd better check all the other wards and there he was curled up in bed with this fifty year old who was also suffering from Alzheimers.

VANESSA. What! A man or a woman.

BETH. A woman, a woman, she was actually quite attractive but she was out to lunch too. It's young isn't it?

(VANESSA TO KITCHEN TABLE TAKES SANDWICH PLATE BACK TO BENCH A. BETH GOES TO SINK LEAVES STAGE OPEN FOR PAT AND VANESSA TO EXCHANGE GLANCES.)

(PAT and VANESSA speak at the same time.)

PAT. Yes.

VANESSA. No.

BETH. Anyhow here they both were curled up together in a single bed.

PAT. Of course institutions won't allow such carryings-on

so he was quickly bundled off to his own bed. Seems silly, doesn't it, at that stage of their lives what does it matter? If they can find creature comforts with each other have it, I say.

VANESSA. That's amazing.

(BETH GETS COCONUT OUT OF CUPBOARD UNDER BENCH B. SHE PUTS COCONUT ON LEMON ICING.)

BETH. Apparently it's quite common. Some of the old dears form strong attachments to each other. One woman told me about her mother who had been a professional woman with an accountancy degree. She went around patting any male on the backside. Doctors and all. When they heard her call 1-2-3 coming ready or not the male patients would shuffle off in the opposite direction and she'd chase after them giggling and shrieking "I'm he, I'm he".

(VANESSA GETS CLOTH FROM SINK AND WIPES HER WORKING AREA.)

PAT. Geriatric chasey. Probably something she wanted to do all her life—you know chase after the fellas—but couldn't. Not the done thing.

BETH. I love one story that Dad's doctor told me. These two old dears, they weren't married but they were continually found in bed together. After about the fifth time the doctor, to try and make the point clear said "Mr. Smith you know there could be serious consequences for Mrs. Brown if you keep hopping into bed with her, she's got acute angina." Mr. Smith replied "I'll say she has." I think it was only a joke but it made me feel better about Dad's behavior.

(BETH WASHES HANDS.)

PAT. *(Laughs loudly.)* I haven't heard that one before. A friend of mine who has a son at university in America, well she wrote and she told me that there was one time just before the election when Bill Clinton visited an older people's home, and there was an old lady there who he was talking to, you know, doing his PR stuff, and he realized that she didn't know who he was. So he asked her. He said "Do you know who I am?" And she looked at him with a smile and said "No, no I'm sorry I don't, but if you ask that lady down there at the desk, she'll be able to tell you. *(They ALL laugh.)* Honestly, Ness, Beth is terrific. Not everyone would have looked after their father the way she has, it's really hard yacka.

(VANESSA PUTS CRUMBS IN BIN WASHES HANDS GOES BACK TO BENCH A WORKING AREA.)

VANESSA. How bad was it? Like... could he do anything for himself?

(BETH PUTS AWAY COCONUT AND COVERS ICING BOWL WITH THE PIECE OF PLASTIC WRAP THAT WAS ORIGINALLY ON IT.)

PAT. No, nothing.
BETH. Towards the end it was like nursing a baby, he couldn't do anything. At the beginning he just used to forget things, then he couldn't read or write, he'd apparently had a series of mini strokes which meant that he'd gradually deteriorate, after each one he'd plateau down a little further until finally I had to spoon feed him.

(PAT SEARCHES FOR SOMETHING ON TOP OF FRIDGE, AROUND SINK.)

VANESSA. Like a little child?

BETH. Yes, he was just eating mush and it would spill all over the place...

VANESSA. Argh!

(BETH PUTS CAKE ON CAKE PLATE, TAKES CAKE TO DINING TABLE.)

BETH. After you feed a baby it'll go to sleep, right? I'd just finish feeding Dad and he'd say "I'm hungry, where's lunch?" He had no sense of time, no short term memory.

(PAT OPENS OVEN.)

PAT. Speaking of short term memory, has anyone seen my oven mitt? *(Finds it in her apron pocket.)* Stop looking, I've found it. The worst part was when he became incontinent.

(PAT PUTS SCONES.)

VANESSA. What do you mean? He used to wet the bed and that?

PAT. Yeah, some of his dirty nappies were beauts. We started cooking bland food for him—definitely no onions.

(BETH ADDS WATER FROM KETTLE TO CHOCOLATE ICING. MIXING ICING SHE SHOWS A SPOONFUL TO AUDIENCE AND VANESSA.)

VANESSA. Yuck, you mean you had to clean that as well.

It's horrible. I can't imagine wiping my father's private parts.
   BETH. You just sort of do it.

(PAT GOES TO SINK, GETS CLOTH.)

   PAT. And it's constant, twenty-four hours a day. You hope
they're going to sleep through the night but...

(BETH UNCOVERS DOUBLE SPONGE, STARTS ICING.)

   BETH. I had this sort of alarm system that we put in his
room that would go off if he opened the door. It was best for
me to sleep when he was sleeping but of course that would be
any time of the night or day.

*(VANESSA MOVES TO TABLE SETS OUT BREAD, STARTS SPREADING
   CURRIED EGG.)*

   VANESSA. Why did you do it?
   BETH. Well, I mean he looked after me when I was little.
   VANESSA. But he had to look after you. I mean he was
your father. That's his obligation. You don't owe him anything.

(PAT WASHES HANDS.)

   BETH. Oh I did, I loved him. And I just did it. I didn't have
any second thoughts about it. He got sick and I just did it. It
seemed the natural thing to do.

(PAT TAKES SMALL BOWL FROM CUPBOARD.)

VANESSA. For five years.

BETH. Yeah, well you don't know how long it is going to go on for.

(PAT PUTS ALL SORTS OF LICORICE IN BOWL.)

PAT. Well it's about five years since he stopped recognizing anyone. Like he hasn't even known you has he?

BETH. No. No-one really.

PAT. Enid thinks he knew her but he didn't, he didn't. Sometimes she'd stay with him when Beth went out and for some reason he always behaved for her. You'd come home and she'd say "When I look after him it's nothing, the dear man slept the whole time—like a baby. I don't know why you find it so difficult."

BETH. Yes, he did sleep for her, the old devil.

VANESSA. She'd put anyone to sleep.

(VANESSA STARTS SPREADING CURRIED EGG. BETH SPREADS CHOC ICING.)

PAT. What about that time when Frances was visiting from South Africa, remember? Beth's sister came home and said... Go on Beth, you tell it.

(PAT TAKES BOWL OF LOLLIES TO TABLE AND STAYS THERE.)

BETH. Well, Frances offered to look after him so that I could go out and have a good time. So I did.

PAT. Yes, she did. And she got home... you weren't late were you?

BETH. No. About twelve-thirty/one o'clock. When I came in Frances said "Oh Beth, this has got to stop, we can't have this going on". I thought great! Terrific! She's seen what it is I have to do day in day out. Then she said "You can't leave him like this, he's been crying for you ever since you left. You shouldn't leave him like this he gets too upset."

VANESSA. What! She couldn't even look after him for one night.

PAT. That's something eh? I really couldn't believe it.

VANESSA. So what about your friends and stuff? Didn't you ever see anybody?

(BETH COVERS ICING AND PUTS IT IN FRIDGE.)

BETH. Oh yeah, friends came round to see me, which was good but they got a bit tired of it after a while. I've still got friends, I haven't cut myself off totally.

PAT. What about Geoff, you cut yourself off there, didn't you?

(BETH GOES TO FRIDGE—GETS CREAM.)

BETH. That wouldn't have worked anyhow.

PAT. Why not?

BETH. Well... Dad...

PAT. Honestly Ness, she hasn't had any social life for ages but now it's a whole new ball game.

VANESSA. Yeah, just think of all the things you can do now, it'll be great. We'll take you out, won't we, Arnie?

PAT. Yeah, of course. Got anything you'd like to do Beth?

BETH. Well, the first thing I'd like to do is go out to a really swish restaurant and then to the theatre.

PAT. Good, we'll do that.

(BETH GOES TO CUPBOARD, GETS JAM, STARTS SPREADING IT ON SPONGE CAKE.)

BETH. And then I think I'll sell the house.

(PAT is hearing this for the first time and is stunned. She is saddened and internalizes her feelings unnoticed by VANESSA and BETH.)

VANESSA. Wow.
BETH. Yeah and go away. See things.
VANESSA. Travel? Great. Where to?

(VANESSA CUTS SANDWICHES.)

BETH. I don't know. I think I'll go up north for a while. Cairns or somewhere like that. Then I'd like to go overseas and backpack around Europe.
VANESSA. Backpack! That sounds like a great idea. There's no point in hanging around.

(PAT GOES TO FRIDGE GETS CARROTS AND CELERY, TAKES PLATTER FROM TOP OF FRIDGE.)

BETH. I want to move on, I've lived here all my life. Dad's lived here all his life. Nothing's changed here for over 50 years. Some young couple can buy it and do it up.
VANESSA. Well, it's a bit like a mausoleum.

(BETH PUTS JAM BACK IN CUPBOARD AND TAKES WALNUTS & CHER-RIES TO TABLE.)

BETH. The only problem is how to tell Enid.

VANESSA. She'll die. She'll absolutely go off the deep end when you tell her you're going.

(VANESSA SETS SANDWICHES ON SANDWICH PLATE.)

BETH. Yes, I have to work out how I'm going to break it to her. I know she is expecting me to stay here and look after her in her old age, isn't she Pat?

PAT. *(Pulls herself together.)* Yes, I suppose she is.

VANESSA. Chuck 'em all into nursing homes, I say. I don't know how you can be bothered with them when they don't even know who you are.

BETH. But you see, that was it. I thought Dad didn't know who I was but that time when my sister looked after him he knew I wasn't around. You just never know what's going on in their minds.

VANESSA. Oh, Beth, looking after your father is one thing but you can't be expected to do it for Enid.

BETH. I know. I'm not going to but she thinks I am.

VANESSA. I'd just set her straight on that one.

PAT. Yes, you'll have to make it clear.

BETH. She certainly hasn't wasted any time dropping hints. I mean Dad's still warm and she's...

VANESSA. Booking you up for her life.

BETH. The next ten years.

VANESSA. Or should I say death. That won't be long she looks like a walking corpse anyway.

(BETH PUTS WALNUTS ON CHOC ICING. PAT CUTS CARROTS AND CELERY INTO STICKS.)

PAT. Vanessa, that's terrible.
VANESSA. Well look at her, she's rotting from the inside.

(BETH laughs.)

BETH. Don't let her catch you saying that.
VANESSA. Well she even smells a bit strange.
PAT. Oh, she does not.
VANESSA. Yes, she does.
PAT. That's lavender water.

(BETH PUTS CHERRIES ON CAKE.)

BETH. It's a real old ladies' smell. I remember old Aunts of mine smelling like that. They use it to cover up body odors.

(VANESSA GOES TO SINK TO GET DISHCLOTH—INTERACTION BE-TWEEN HER AND PAT. GOES BACK TO WIPE TABLE.)

VANESSA. Yes, an old Aunt of mine smells like that, stale and musty.

(PAT and ENID speak the next two lines overlapping.)

PAT. Get out of here. Shhh! Here she comes!
ENID. Yoo hoo!

(ENID PLACES BRANDY BOTTLE ON TABLE, WASHES HANDS.)

ENID. *(Entering ready for work with sleeve protector, apron and brandy.)* I'm back with the brandy. I had a little taste just to see if it was all right. And it is. It's wonderful.

PAT. You wicked woman, you, Enid. You'll never get to Heaven.

ENID. Now, what would you like me to do?

VANESSA. You could help me cut these sandwiches, I'd really appreciate that.

(ENID TAKES TEATOWEL FROM DRAWER IN TABLE.)

ENID. Well first of all you should put down a tea-towel then the breadboard so that you can collect all the crumbs after you cut them. I always cut them this way in triangles, alternating the color of the bread. Is that all right?

(VANESSA GOES TO DRESSER FOR SANDWICH TRAY.)

PAT. Enid do it however you like.

ENID. Well I just thought I'd ask. Some people get really upset if things aren't done the way they're used to.

(ENID CUTS SANDWICHES.)

VANESSA. Yeah, you know it's true. People can get very strange in someone else's kitchen. They ask how to do the simplest things. Like will I butter the bread thick or thin? Or how do you cut your oranges? Silly things that they'd do automatically in their own home.

(VANESSA TAKES PARSLEY FROM SHELF ABOVE SINK.)

PAT. Yes, I even do that in my own kitchen when there's someone helping me. What do you suppose that is? Self doubt? Or the desire to please?

(PAT laughs.)

(BETH - PRETENDS TO - ADD BRANDY TO CREAM, WITH BACK TO AUDIENCE AT BENCH, RETURNS TO TABLE AND WHISKS CREAM.)

VANESSA. It's the same thing, isn't it?
PAT. Yes, that's right.
ENID Well if you don't want the sandwiches this way, why don't you just say so. It's no skin off my nose.
PAT. Enid that's not what I'm saying.

(Long pause as WOMEN work away.)

(PAT TAKES DIPS FROM FRIDGE. VANESSA PUTS PARSLEY ON SANDWICHES ON DINING TABLE.)

BETH. *(To VANESSA.)* Have you finished your course yet?
VANESSA. Nearly. Two more assignments and I'm through.
BETH. Great. What are you going to do? Teach?
VANESSA. I don't know. Probably not. I didn't like doing my teaching rounds, I don't think I could stand the kids. Little shits.

(BETH PUTS BOTTOM LAYER OF CAKE ON CAKE STAND. SPREADS CREAM.)

BETH. They give you a bad time?

VANESSA. Some of them did. If I thought I could teach them something then I might consider it, but most of them don't seem to want to learn.

(PAT WASHES HANDS, STARTS TO LOOK FOR BISCUITS.)

ENID. Well in my day, we learned to cook at home from our mothers. School was for reading, writing and 'rithmetic.

(ENID CLEANS UP TABLE. PAT OPENS CUPBOARDS LOOKING FOR DRY BISCUITS.)

VANESSA. Home economics isn't only cooking Enid. You have to know food analysis, lots of biological and health stuff, nutrition, human development, there's heaps to learn. But the kids aren't interested. All they can think about is getting to the toilets for a smoke, or to Macdonalds for a hamburger.

PAT. Bloody little devils!

VANESSA. The boys are the worst. You can already see a pattern forming.

ENID. Boys cooking?

VANESSA. The girls want to work, but they can't because boys disrupt the class and demand attention. Then when they fall behind with their work, they ask the girls to do it for them.

PAT. Where did you put the dry biscuits?

BETH. Up there, in the flour tin.

PAT. Silly me, what were you saying 'Ness?

(PAT MOVES STOOL OVER TO KITCHEN TO STAND ON TO GET FLOUR TIN.)

VANESSA. Often the silly little things do it too—even though they complain. Why do they do it? It's the same with my catering job. The women do all the work, and the men get all the credit. It's like you nursing your Dad, Beth. What acknowledgment do you get for that? It's hard work, it's underrated and you don't even get paid. Men expect and get everything.

BETH. Vanessa, it's not a matter of what sex the person is. If it had been my mother who was ill I'd have done the same thing for her.

(PAT SETS BISCUITS ON PLATTER WITH CARROTS AND DIPS AT BENCH.)

VANESSA. I suppose you would. But how many men would nurse their mothers. I would like to see a group of men in the kitchen making sandwiches like we are. It's not that they can't, it's that they won't. Unless they get paid for it.

(ENID AND BETH CLEAR KITCHEN TABLE.)

PAT. Or they're hungry. I must admit, it's hard to imagine a bunch of fellas working in a kitchen. Sure they'd make a sandwich, but its hard to picture them icing cakes.

ENID. They wouldn't work as fast or as co-operatively as we do at something like this—but well I wouldn't have been able to do what Jack used to do when he was a bank manager.

(ENID SETS ENAMEL WATER BOWL ON TOP OF DISHCLOTH ON FRONT CORNER OF THE TABLE. BETH TAKES CHOCOLATE CAKE TO D TABLE THEN RETURNS TO TABLE FOR LINE UP. PAT PICKS UP DIP PLATTER AND DISPLAYS IT TO BETH AND ENID SO THAT

THEY END UP IN A LINE BEHIND TABLE WITH BETH STAGE RIGHT, PAT CENTER, ENID STAGE LEFT.)

VANESSA. Well I could. The catering form I work for want me to become their functions manager when I finish. In three years or so I'll be running my own business. I don't want to get stuck in that dreary, domestic rut so many women find themselves in. Look at the three of you. Look to the right and you see a version of yourself 20 years ago. *(They ALL look to person Stage Right of them.)* Look the other way—20 years ahead? I'm not going to spend the rest of my life in a routine like that.

(BETH turns and looks at PAT, PAT then looks at ENID who in turn looks at the oven.)

VANESSA. *(Unconscious of the consternation she has created.)* How are we going to set up the cups and saucers? Do you want them on the tea trolley?

(PAT PUTS FLOUR TIN BACK.)

PAT. That's probably the best way.

VANESSA. There's going to be a lot of washing up.

PAT. I wouldn't worry too much about that, guests always help out with that especially at funerals. Just hand them an apron and a tea towel and they'll hop into it.

(BETH TAKES SCONE BASKET FROM TOP OF FRIDGE SETS CLOTH IN IT PUTS IT ON TOP OF STOVE. VANESSA SETS CUP ON TROLLEY.)

VANESSA. That's the worst part of the catering jobs. The cleaning up.

ENID. Do you cater for many funerals?
VANESSA. No, most people do their own I think.

(PAT PUTS STOOL BACK NEXT TO STOVE WITH THE BOWL OF MIX ON TOP.)

PAT. Clever!
VANESSA. You know what I mean.

(PAT TAKES DIP PLATTER TO TABLE.)

PAT. Our church committee does them sometimes. I helped at a few and I kept seeing this same old guy turning up at all the funerals and getting pissed. I thought it was really sad that he was losing all his friends and rellies until I discovered he was a professional mourner.
ENID. A what?
PAT. A professional mourner. Apparently he'd read the funeral notices every day, and if a Rotarian or a Mason or a Lion, any lodge member had died he'd put on the appropriate badge, go to the service and get asked back to the house. He was permanently pissed for weeks on end without having to buy one drink.
BETH. Would anyone like a drink, a sherry or something?

(BETH crosses to dresser.)

ENID. I just might have another sip of my hospital brandy.
BETH. Doing you the power of good, is it Enid?
PAT. Oops, I'll just have to go out to the line and see if my gloves are dry.

(PAT exits.)

VANESSA. What did she say?
BETH. Don't you know that story of Pat's?

(ENID POURS HERSELF A DRINK. BETH CROSSES TO DRESSER.)

VANESSA. No.
BETH. Well just after Pat got married, her mother-in-law...
VANESSA. My Nan?
BETH. Yeah.
VANESSA. That stupid, stuck-up old thing?

*(BETH POURS DRINK FOR HERSELF AND VANESSA. HANDS VANESSA
DRINK DURING FOLLOWING.)*

BETH. Well, she came to stay with her. Pat didn't know a
lot about cooking, but to make the big impression, she tried
all sorts of exotic dishes using spices, garlic, onions etc., and
apparently it filled her mother-in-law with gas. She was a gen-
teel sort of lady who wore white gloves when she went out
and so she washed them all the time. Well whenever she wanted
to break wind she wouldn't do it in company, she'd bottle it
up when she couldn't hold it in any longer she'd say "I'll just
go out to the line to see if my gloves are dry". So that's what
Pat's doing now. Cheers!

(BETH and VANESSA clink glasses.)

ENID. Beth you haven't made any sardine sandwiches.
BETH. I know and I'm not going to.

(BETH CLOSES DRESSER DOORS.)

ENID. But you can't have a funeral without sardine sandwiches, everyone has them.

BETH. Yes, they're the ones that are always left on the plate with the limp piece of parsley.

ENID. Well I don't know what people will think if we don't have them.

BETH. For God's sake Enid what does it matter. No-one is going to notice.

(VANESSA GOES TO SINK—WASHES GLASS AND HANDS.)

VANESSA. Why do they have them at funerals anyway, is there some symbolic significance or something.

ENID. Oh I don't know. I just know you have them. It's the done thing.

BETH. *(Exasperated.)* Enid!

(PAT re-enters.)

PAT. That's better.

VANESSA. Arnie Pat! *(VANESSA spills a bowl of liquid.)* Oh, I'm sorry how on earth did I do that?

(VANESSA GOES TO K TABLE TAKES DISH CLOTH - ENID HAS PRESET THIS UNDER BOWL - SPILLING IQUID ONTO FLOOR AND ON ENID.)

PAT. Don't worry about it Vanessa. Beth, have you got a mop?

(VANESSA GOES TO D TABLE.)

BETH. Yes, I'll just get it.

(BETH exits.)

(PAT TAKES SCONES OUT OF OVEN. ENID WASHES HANDS AND DRIES THEM AT SINK AND SPONGES HERSELF DRY.)

VANESSA. Arnie, the table is starting to look good isn't it. *(No response from PAT.)* Do you think we will have enough? *(Pause.)* Arnie Pat?
     PAT. Yes?
     VANESSA. Are you all right?
     PAT. Yes, yes I was just away with the fairies. *(Pause.)* I didn't realize that Beth'd be leaving that's all.

(PAT CROSSES OVER TO VANESSA AT DINING TABLE.)

VANESSA. What did you expect her to do? I think it's a great idea for her to pack up and leave. What's left for her here?
     ENID. Who's leaving? *(Pause.)* I said, who's leaving?
     VANESSA. *(Changing the subject.)* I think that plate needs some parsley don't you?
     PAT. Yes, yes it does.
     ENID. Will you answer my question?
     VANESSA. *(Cornered.)* Oh. Um. Well I shouldn't be telling you this Enid. But Beth's leaving. She wants to tell you herself so it would be good if you didn't let on that I told you.

ENID. Beth!?! What's she doing? Where's she going?

VANESSA. I knew I shouldn't have said anything. She's going away.

ENID. Away? Away, where? Off on a holiday?

VANESSA. No, not for a holiday. She said that she was going to sell the house and move away.

ENID. But she didn't ask me.

VANESSA. I beg your pardon?

ENID. She didn't ask me, I don't know anything about this.

(PAT MOVES TO SINK—WASHES HANDS.)

PAT. No, she didn't ask you Enid, as a matter of fact she didn't even discuss it with me, actually.

VANESSA. *(To ENID.)* Why should she ask you?

ENID. Well... I mean... I'm part of the family. I've known her since before she was born. I've been a second mother to her. I always advise her on everything.

PAT. Yes but Enid, how often does she take your advice?

ENID. Often... always.

PAT. Enid you're always handing out, but does she want it? Really, think about it.

ENID. Well I always give her good advice. She's never objected. It's unbelievable, it's downright rude that she should go and make this decision without consulting me.

PAT. Has it ever occurred to you that it's because you are always interfering that she wants to go. You're probably the reason she's decided to move.

ENID. What do you mean by that?

PAT. Oh nothing, nothing—I shouldn't have said it.

*(PAT MOVES TO STOVE TAKES SCONES OUT OF IRONS, PUTS THEM
  IN BASKET.)*

ENID. No you shouldn't. I'm hurt. And I'm angry that she should do this.

VANESSA. Enid there is no reason for her to hang around now that her father's dead.

ENID. Fancy Beth doing this to me.

(ENID sits at K table.)

VANESSA. For heaven's sake, she isn't doing anything to you, she's doing something for herself. It's her life. She's got to move on.

PAT. I don't think it's a good time to sell.

ENID. She's being utterly selfish.

VANESSA. She's being selfish? *(To ENID.)* What do you expect her to do? What you want her to do.

ENID. She's just thinking of herself. Just thinking of herself.

VANESSA. She wants to leave and there is nothing you can do to keep her here.

ENID. But what will happen to her?

PAT. Enid, how old do you think she is?

ENID. She's always lived here. She's needed me every day to help her with Jack and everything.

VANESSA. Enid Jack doesn't need you anymore and I'm sure Beth can do without you. What you're worried about is can you do without her.

(ENID does not absorb this but PAT does.)

(Re-enter BETH carrying bucket and mop—PAT takes mop from BETH.)

PAT. Here I'll do that.

(BETH MOVES TO SINK AND WASHES AND DRIES HANDS.)

BETH. Thanks. I've got some nuts and chips that I mustn't forget to put out. Enid could you give me the salad bowl?

(ENID RISES WITH CONTROLLED ANGER AND GETS BOWL FROM BENCH CUPBOARD AND PLACES IT EMPHATICALLY ON BENCH A. RETURNS WITH OUTRAGED DIGNITY TO CHAIR AT TABLE. BETH EMPTIES CHIPS INTO BOWL AND PUTS CHIP PACKET ON BENCH.)

BETH. *(Cont. Offering chips to VANESSA.)* Want some?
VANESSA. *(Avoiding eye contact.)* No thanks.

(BETH TAKES CHIPS TO TABLE.)

BETH. I turned on the party pies while I was out there. That OK? *(Pause—BETH becomes aware of the stony silence.)* What's wrong?
ENID. *(Unable to contain her anger any longer.)* What's this I hear?
BETH. I beg your pardon?
ENID. Why didn't you tell me you were going away?
VANESSA. I'm sorry Beth... I just er... ah... told Enid about your plans to sell up.
BETH. You did what?

VANESSA. It was an accident really. Pat was...

BETH. Vanessa. How dare you. You come in here, into my house and start interfering. You knew I was having trouble thinking how I should tell Enid. It's all very well for you to come in here helping out, oh very nice, very kind, but for God's sake stick to buttering the bread will you, and keep your mouth shut.

PAT. Look honestly Beth it was my fault. I was thinking about you going and I started to talk about it. I sort of didn't register that Enid was listening., It was my fault. Don't go mad at Vanessa.

VANESSA. Auntie Pat.

PAT. *(Continuing.)* She wasn't to blame. Come on Beth. Look I know you're upset about your Dad but try not to take it out on Vanessa. O.K.

BETH. I'm sorry. Yes, you're right. I'm sorry.

(PAT MOPS FLOOR. VANESSA TAKES SAUCE AND JUG FROM CUP-BOARD.)

ENID. Why didn't you tell me?

BETH. Enid I wasn't keeping anything from you. It's just a decision that I've made and as yet I hadn't had a chance to tell you. I was concerned about how I was going to break it to you. Its unfortunate you found out the way you did but it doesn't change the fact that I'm going.

ENID. But you didn't ask me dear.

(VANESSA PUTS SAUCE IN JUG.)

BETH. Why should I ask you. It's not your house, it's not your decision. It is my decision, I don't have to ask you anything.

ENID. To think I should have found out through somebody else.

PAT. Are you sure you know what you want to do?

BETH. Yes. I know I need to get away.

PAT. Well why not try a holiday, it doesn't mean you have to sell up does it?

BETH. Yes, it does. I can't go on a holiday and feel free knowing all the time that I have to come back to this house and its past. I'm making a complete and utter break. Don't you see? At long last Dad has died and given both of us our freedom.

ENID. How can you say such a thing.

BETH. Well it's true. I've been shackled to this shell of a person for years, we all have, and now we are free, all of us, to do anything we like. Don't you understand, I'm glad that he's dead.

(PAT moves towards door with bucket and mop.)

ENID. Beth dear, I don't think you're entirely well, The funeral has been a strain on you. Of course you're not glad he's dead.

BETH. Oh yes I am. *(PAT stops at door.)* I know that will shock you Enid, with your old fashioned sense of values, and I know that everyone expects me to be distraught. But I'm not. All I feel is an overwhelming sense of relief. Oh I know I have to go through the pantomime of this wake. They'll all come tramping through the house looking at everything, pricing it as they go, figuring out how much I'm worth. *(Acts out the following.)* "Oh Beth I'm so sorry about your father, you'll miss him." "Good old Jack. He was a great guy. I can remember when I was a little chap how he used to pretend that china dog was alive, you know and he'd bark at me. If ever you think you want to sell it, let me know." "My condolences Beth, it's a sad time. You won't know yourself now with so much time on your hands. You'll have to find an interest so that you don't get depressed." Oh yes they'll all be offering sympathy and advice—you know 'helping' me. But where was the support and practical help when I was really needing it. When I was watching my wonderful Dad mentally die and turn into a vacant shell, where were all the friends and rellies then? Did they visit? Did they put the odd casserole in the freezer to help me manage? They stayed away in droves. Now they're all appeasing their consciences with a 'duty' funeral appearance. Dad died years ago. I've already done my grieving. *(She sees empty chip packet on bench.)* Saying good-bye today was as meaningless as throwing away an empty chip packet. I am glad he's dead, do you hear—GLAD, and I don't want you to expect me to feel guilty about it.

(PAT exits with bucket and mop.)

ENID. Well we won't talk any more about it now, we'll wait until tomorrow, after you've had a good sleep, you'll be your old self again.

(PAT REENTERS AND INDICATES TO VANESSA TO GET BREAD BOARDS FROM SINK. VANESSA FETCHES AND TAKES BOARDS TO KITCHEN TABLE.)

BETH. *(Decisively.)* No, I am not going back to my old self. It's time for a change, it's time for all of us to change. We've been using him as an excuse not to get on with our own lives.

(PAT has re-entered.)

(PAT TAKES GEM IRONS FROM TOP OF OVEN. STANDS HOLDING THEM FOR A MOMENT.)

ENID. But that is what our life is for. What we've been doing is what a woman does. The purpose of our being is to nurture and care for our loved ones.

BETH. Enid, is that what you really believe. You poor sad thing, you know what I'm thinking? You've spent your whole life doing your 'nurturing and caring' for a family who didn't need it. An unwilling, substitute family.

(Pause.)

(PAT DROPS GEM IRONS ON TO BREAD BOARDS)

ENID. *(Angrily.)* Give me back my bottle of brandy.

(ENID acts as if she is about to leave.)

(VANESSA - DISCREETLY - PUTS SAUCE ON THE BACK OF HER DRESS—NOT TO BE REVEALED TO AUDIENCE. PAT STEPS INTO ENID'S WAY, NODS TO THE BRANDY.)

PAT. Hang on Ee! I could do with one of those now. Could you give me a glass Beth? *(Crosses toward BETH at the dresser. Aside astonishment.)* A bit severe I thought.

Here Ee. Give us the bottle—anyone else want one? *(PAT crosses to dresser to get glasses then pours drink for ENID.)* OK Ee say when. *(No 'when' from ENID, glass gets quite full. PAT also pours one for herself.)* Here's to our future life.

(ENID swallows whole drink and gasps.) It seems it is going to be quite different.

ENID. *(Slightly tipsy by this time.)* You know Pat, I've been thinking about what Beth said, and trying to understand it. It seems to me that she's saying I've wasted my whole life.

PAT. No, I'm sure she doesn't mean that.

ENID. Oh yes she does, and you know something, she's right. Well look at me. A lonely old woman, who has never done a thing in her life. What have I got to show for my 72 years. Nothing. And it's not because I've failed. It's because I haven't even tried. When I was young I used to dream I'd be another Amelia Earhardt fly planes and that. Jack told me that I was mad "a woman's place was in the home", he said.

(PAT GETS BUTTER FROM FRIDGE AND KNIFE FROM DRAWER IN BENCH A, AND SITS AT K TABLE PUTTING BUTTER IN GEM IRONS.)

PAT. That'd be right.

ENID. *(Pause.)* I loved him you know, ever since I was a kid. When he married Faye it broke my heart. I married Reg on the rebound, he was a pilot and flying always fascinated me, and when he got shot down in the war, well Jack, Faye and the girls became my family, as Beth said—my unwilling, substitute family. *(BETH and PAT exchange glances.)* I was 59 when your mother died, I thought Jack would marry me then, but he didn't. Not long after that he became ill so I helped nurse him. What else could I do? I've lived my whole life trying to please him and now I'm an old woman who has done nothing.

PAT and BETH uncomfortable—VANESSA comes to the rescue.)

VANESSA. Come on, Enid your life isn't over yet. Knowing your stamina you could go for at least another twenty-five years, There's plenty of time to do something.

ENID. Yeah—what?

VANESSA. What would you like to do?

ENID. Fly a plane. They wouldn't let me do that now though.

PAT. No. I think you've left that a bit late.

ENID. Oh but I loved being up there. Reg took me up a few times in a little plane. I wanted to jump out, I would of too if I'd had a parachute. Imagine drifting down, seeing forever.

VANESSA. Why don't you do it then?

ENID. What?

VANESSA. Parachute jump.

PAT. Oh come Ness.

ENID. What? Oh I couldn't.

VANESSA. Why couldn't you, you're fit and healthy. You don't have to do it by yourself you know. I think an instructor or someone jumps out with you.

ENID. What? He carries you all the way down, like Superman?

PAT. Does he, Ness? Well we could find out, couldn't we. Look I reckon you can do almost anything at any age. I was watching the telly the other night and they had a granny abseiling down a cliff and she was loving every mᴖᴗute of it. You could give that a go too Ee.

ENID. Yes. I've always wanted to fly free like a bird. And if I don't do it soon I might never get the chance.

VANESSA. If you take it up seriously, I bet you could get jobs on commercials. You know—Little Old Lady racing to the rescue, or delivering mail or something like that.

ENID. I wonder if I could. *(Singing.)* "I'll fly through the air with the greatest of ease In the arms of the man with the parachute, please".

(ENID twirls her way across the stage. BETH catches her and sits her down at dining table.)

PAT. What about bungi jumping? Ee how about giving that a go?

VANESSA. So you two are both going off with packs on your backs. I thought you were sick of burdens.

(BETH hugs ENID who is feeling dizzy.)

BETH. As long as I don't have to jump out of a plane nursing Enid.

PAT GOES TO STOVE, GETS SPOONS AND SPOON REST, PUTS THEM ON TABLE AND GOES BACK FOR GEM MIX.)

PAT. Well it looks like things'll be much quieter around here. Still there's always Mrs. Benson she'll probably be needing a hand with her mother. And of course there's Christine Northey.

BETH. Oh come on Pat. What about you? You're always helping other people. When are you going to do something for yourself?

VANESSA. Yeah Arnie...

PAT. I don't know, Beth, I don't know. *(Pause.)* You're going to cringe when I say this Ness, but well, I enjoy helping people. Working as a team. Like we did for Jack. It's like Enid said—it's what a woman does—nurturing and caring, but these days the people who do those things are made to feel inadequate, *(Defiant.)* but I like it. I get pleasure from it.

VANESSA. Well why don't you do a course in Social Work. Then you could get a job and get paid for doing what you're doing now for nothing.

PAT. Ah I see—having a title and getting paid for it makes something worthwhile. Doing the same thing for the love of it makes it worthless.

VANESSA. That's not what I mean.

PAT. Vanessa, I don't want to go and study for three years to learn what I do already. God they have classes now for the craziest things. I believe you can go and learn how to be a mother. There are classes to teach you how to enjoy yourself. How to teach you children to play. How to cry. How to love. How to breathe. Hey! I haven't seen anything yet on how to defecate, but I'll bet there is one. What's wrong with just living? What's wrong with responding naturally. Why should I feel I have to apologize for it? *(She looks at everyone staring at her outburst.)* Oh, I'm sorry.

(PAT TAKES GEM MIX TO TABLE AND STARTS FILLING GEM IRONS.)

VANESSA. *(Realizes she has sat on some tomato sauce, jumping up and removing apron.)* Oh no, oh look at my skirt. Or Arnie Pat I can't serve tea in this. People will think that I've got my... you know...

PAT. Got your period. Well it does look like it. Come here Vanessa.

ENID. *(Dryly.)* I should be so lucky.

*(PAT THROWS APRON TO ENID AND STARTS WASHNG SPOT ON
VANESSA'S SKIRT.*

PAT. *(Looks at ENID and starts laughing.)* Oh Enid what a
funny thing for you to say.

ENID. *(Putting on the french maid apron.)* How does this
look?

*(ENID dances and sings a drunken can can. The others laugh
and watch her making appropriate comments.)*

BETH. Come with me Vanessa, I've probably got something you can change into.

ENID. *(Following BETH and VANESSA.)* Oh yes there's
that nice... dress I put in your wardrobe the other day, the one
I brought back from the dry cleaners.

(BETH, VANESSA and ENID exit.)

*(AFTER WASHING HER HANDS, PAT BEGINS FILLING GEM IRONS WITH
GEM MIX, HUMMING A SAD CAN CAN.)*

*(BETH enters and watches PAT for a moment—PAT is hum-
ming a sad Can Can as she works.)*

BETH. You never stop do you? Would you like a cup of
tea?

PAT. Is the Pope a Catholic? No, I'll wait now till everyone's
here. Want to give me a hand?

(BETH WIPES HANDS, GETS SPOONS FROM DRAWER THEN STARTS TO HELP PAT WITH GEM MIX.)

BETH. Sure. Enid's helping Vanessa try on a few of my outfits to see if they fit, they may not be her style though.

PAT. Beth... *(Pause.)* Are you really going to sell up and go?

BETH. Aha.

PAT. So you're going to leave us. It never occurred to me that you would do that. It's a bit of a shock you know.

BETH. You must have known with Dad dead that things would change.

PAT. Yes I did, but some how I thought that I'd be a part of it. Thought, you know, that we'd go to movies and theatre and that, but we'd see each other have a cuppa everyday like we've always done. I suppose I thought you'd always be here.

BETH. I'll still see you, I'll come and visit.

PAT. Of course, but it won't be the same.

BETH. Heh, I'm not disappearing off the face of the earth. I'll be around for a while yet, you can't get rid of me that easily. I just don't want to live the rest of my life in this house. I have to try a few things while I can. I thought you'd understand that Pat.

PAT. I do, I do. It's just that, well, I'm going to miss you.

BETH. I'll miss you too. You know how much I've relied on you for support. I wouldn't have been able to do it without you. But thank God, it's over now.

(THEY FINISH FILLING THE GEM IRONS.)

PAT. Yes, it's over... and you're right, you do have to make changes, but you know how you said you didn't want to feel guilty about being glad Jack's dead—well right now, for some absurd reason, I'm feeling guilty because I'm wishing he was still alive.

(PAT is close to tears.)

BETH. Oh Pat—I'm so stupid. All along I thought it would be Enid who'd get upset.

(PAT and BETH give each other a big hug.)

PAT. I'd better get these gems in the oven. Are you all right to clean up here? I just need to go and freshen up.

(BETH OPENS OVEN DOOR, PAT PUTS GEMS IN OVEN AND EXITS. BETH CLEANS K TABLE FINALLY FINDING THE CARNATION. SHE TAKES IT TO THE DRESSER...)

(BETH removes photo of JACK from dresser.)

BETH. *(To photo.)* Good-bye Dad.

(BETH hugs photo, returns it to dresser and places carnation in front of it.)

(Lights fade to Black.)

Epilogue

(Lights up for Graveside.)

JIM. *(To Congregation.)* All of us are here today because of one common link—Jack. Some of you have known him for many years and remember him as the friend and gentleman he was. Those of you who knew him in his capacity as bank manager will have paid off the mortgages long ago. But there is no doubt that you will recall the kindness, courtesy and discretion with which he handled your affairs. Those of you who have only known Jack in his last years may not know the qualities he showed as a parent to his two daughters, Frances and Elizabeth or as we know her Beth. But you all know what wonderful girls they are and that in itself is the greatest testament that could be made to JOHN FRANCIS BLACKBURN. Jack in his illness has been lost to us mentally for some time and so in many ways we are not here to mourn him. Instead let us celebrate his life and the life he has engendered to his children and say good-bye only to that part of Jack that could die. *(Pray.)* For as much as it hath pleased Almighty God of His great mercy to take unto himself the soul of our dear brother here departed we therefore commit his body to the ground; earth to earth, ashes to ashes; dust to dust in sure and certain hope of the Resurrection to Eternal Life through our Lord Jesus Christ, Amen. Those of you who knew Jack's ardent support of his football team will appreciate the request for the final hymn. The words are in your order of service. Please feel free to join in the singing lead by_____.

(Lights up to half house.)

SINGER. "When the Saints Go Marching In".
JIM. Ladies and gentlemen, that concludes the service. It is comforting to see so many of Beth's friends and relations

here to support her in her hour of need, and I daresay many of you will be wondering what has happened to her. Rest assured—all is well. She is at the house waiting for you all to come back for some light refreshments. I'm sure you'll want to extend your sympathy to her and perhaps have a cup of... *(He is interrupted by SINGER who proffers a plate of sardine sandwiches. To SINGER.)* Oh thank you. *(To AUDIENCE.)* Some sardine sandwiches. Appropriate, don't you think, the fish being the symbol for Christ in whom we find everlasting life. Please come this way.

END OF PLAY

AT THE CHURCH

ENTRANCE HYMN
>Amazing Grace

GREETING

READING
>From Isaiah 25:6 - 9

RESPONSORIAL PSALM
>Crimond

READING
>From the First Letter of St. Paul to the Thessalonians

THE BLESSING

RECESSIONAL HYMN   The Lord is My Shepherd

>The Lord's my shepherd I'll not want
>He makes me down to lie
>In pastures green he leadeth me
>The quiet waters by.

>My soul he doth restore again
>And me to walk doth make
>Within the paths of righteousness
>E'en for his own name sake.

>Yea though I walk through death's dark vale
>Yet will I fear no ill
>For thou art with me and thy rod
>And staff me comfort still.

>My table thou has furnished
>In presence of my foes
>My head thou dost with oil anoint

An my cup overflows.

Goodness and mercy all my life
Shall surely follow me
And in God's house forever more
My dwelling place shall be.

AT THE GRAVESIDE

EULOGY
FINAL HYMN When the Saints Go Marching In

We are trav'ling in the footsteps
Of those who've gone before,
But we'll all be reunited
On a new and sunlit shore.

Oh, when the Saints go marching in,
Oh, when the Saints go marching in,
I want to be in that number,
Oh, when the Saints go marching in.

(And when the) sun begins to shine,
And when the sun begins to shine,
I want to be in that number,
When the sun begins to shine.

(And when the) trumpet sounds a call,
Oh when the trumpet sounds a call,
I want to be in that number,

When the trumpet sounds a call.

Some say this world of trouble
Is the only one we need,
But I'm waiting for that morning
When the new world is revealed.

Oh, when the Saints go marching in,
Oh, when the Saints go marching in,
I want to be in that number,
Oh, when the Saints go marching in.

AMEN

PROPERTY LIST

<u>On Top of Oven (pre-heated)</u>
Oven mitts
Pre-greased gem irons x 4
Spoon rest

Fridge
Cheese and celery mixture in bowl
Curried egg mixture in bowl
Whipped cream in small bowl
Whipped cream in large bowl
Milk in Jug
Softened margarine
Dips x 2 in small bowls
3 carrot and 3 sticks of celery in colander
Cheese cubes (biscuit size)
Milk 3 ltrs

Shelf Above Sink
Licorice All sorts
Soap in soap dish
Drinking glass
Metal bowl
Orange squeezer and 2 lemons
Utensils in pot including:
          knives
          sharp knife for carrot cutting
          dessert spoons
          spatula
          whisk

Parsley in a glass of water
Tea caddy
Hand towel on rail
Other period decorations, e.g.
        Australian tin
        Australian calendar
        Salt celler

Top Shelf

Flour tin containing dry biscuits
Other decorations, e.g.
        Canisters
        Weighing scales
        Casserole dish
        pot plant
        preserved fruit

Sink and Bench Surface

Bread boards
Chux x 4
Hot, soapy water in sink
Power point
Electric jug (1/3 full of water)
Tea cup and saucer
Tea pot
Tea strainer
Cupboard by Fridge
Coconut, glace cherries, walnuts, jam
Tomato sauce in bottle
Small jug

<u>Cupboard in Island Bench</u>
Drawer
       utensils
       tea towels
Cups and saucers
Wooden bowl for chips
<u>Dresser</u>
Photo of Jack
Sherry glasses and decanter
Cups and saucers
Otherbdecorative items, e.g.
       plates
       tea set
<u>Dresser Drawer</u>
Table cloths x 2
Cake servers - silver
<u>Lower Cupboard of Dresser</u>
Cups and sucers
Cake stand
Nuts in bowl
Sandwich tray - silver
<u>Dining Table</u>
Bowl of flowers

PERSONAL PROPERTY LIST

Priest - Father Jim
Prayer book
Floral tribute cards

Enid
Handbag
Gloves
Beret
White carnation
Handkerchief
Order of service
Sleeve protectors
Apron
Bottle of brandy

Pat
Basket containing:
> bowl of gem scone mix
> Recipe
>> 4 eggs
>> 4 cups milk
>> 130 gs butter
>> 4 teaspoons sugar
>> 6 cups self raising flour
>> 2 cups sultanas
>
> aprons x 2
> cheese platter
> plate of asparagus rolls
> tea pots x 2

Vanessa
Loaves of bread x 1 pre-buttered, white and brown
Bowl of lemon icing
Bowl of chocolate icing
Sandwich platters x 4
Sponge cakes, one lemon, one double chocolate

Beth
Handbag
Order of service

Floorplan of Set

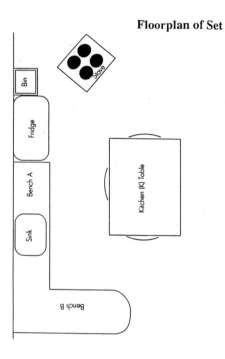

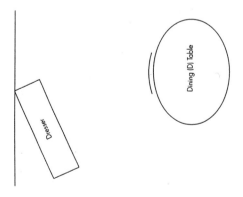

Audience